THE ABYSSAL BIBLE

REV. CAIN

This book is a work of religious nature, and the information herein is intended solely for educational purposes.

You are responsible for yourself, your actions, and how you conduct yourself as a human being – not us, and not anyone else.

Act responsibly, and conduct yourself in a way that exemplifies honor, integrity, and decency towards yourself and those around you.

AUTHOR'S PREFACE

It was many strange and foggy years ago that I first envisioned the faith-philosophy of Aphotism – my hybrid addition to the Left-Hand Path that seeks to unite the long-warring goliaths of science and faith through the worship and celebration of the void. In my pursuit of this daunting goal, I have written the manuscript that you now hold – *The Abyssal Bible*.

It has been my experience as a lifelong practitioner of the occult that the void is rarely discussed at any serious depth – when she *does* make an appearance in one's studies or conversations, she is typically a cursory footnote rather than the rightful star of the show. For countless centuries and still today, there has been a self-imposed deprivation of knowledge and power amongst most occultists – by those who seek the blessings of gods, demons, and deities but never think to explore, praise, or celebrate she who created the creators – our cosmic mother, *the void*.

I believe that this general lack of observance of the void is a matter of naivety – of occultists either not understanding the nature of the void or not having a source to consult that they deem relevant to their lives and/or studies upon the Left-Hand Path. With *The Abyssal Bible,* I address and resolve this age-old dilemma by offering readers a manuscript that highlights the all-powerful divinity of the void and establishes a religion that worships her monarchy.

On the Left-Hand Path of Aphotism, we believe in the dominion of the void – that *nothing* could exist without her, including the most powerful gods and deities that you can name. Christianity's God, the Devil, Abaddon, Apophis, Thanatos – there exists no god, goddess, spirit, or horror unbeholden to the will of the void. Though she may not interfere with the edicts of omniscient beings, it is **because** of the void that these divine beings are permitted to exist.

The void deserves our recognition, reverence, and exploration – to be celebrated as both the paint that all life is designed with and the canvas upon which said life is brought into existence. The void is not only the architect, but the engineer – she is the ship and the sea. She is the divine orchestrator of *every*

instance of life within her infinite, ever-expanding universes – gods, devils, and humans, all the same.

However you decide to incorporate Aphotism into your life and Left-Hand Path, it is my hope that the void becomes an integral part of your journey. For the occultist who embraces the divinity of the void, her transcendental fruits may be devoured without end – the knowledge, power, magic, and secrets of creation itself that are normally reserved for *gods*.

Go forward, and plunge into the cold, black depths of *The Abyssal Bible* – allow the gelid ichor of the void to embalm your mind and soul as you prepare to explore one of the most *electrifying* additions to the Left-Hand Path that has arisen within in the last hundred years – the faith-philosophy of Aphotism.

– Rev. Cain
Indianapolis, IN

TO OUR COSMIC MOTHER, THE VOID.

OMNISCIENT ARCHITECT OF THE DIVINE,

WHOSE BREATH GIVES ASSENT TO ALL LIGHT AND DARKNESS,

REVEREND CAIN WISHES GLORY, HEREIN, UNTO
THE LIMINAL SEAS OF ETERNITY.

Everlasting are the fruits of our abyssal mother, the void – grand architect of existence, engineer of our universe, and creator of all mortals and immortals.

Breathless are the stars of her dreamscape sea – the *inextinguishable* embers of lifeless souls, each one smoldering with anticipation for their turn to live, create, perish, and be reborn again within the void.

In celebration of the void, I honor the path that lies ahead, illuminated by the haunted light of a million deathless moons – bless me, o' cosmic mother, and guide this Aphotist to the bounties of your throne!

THE NAMES AND ORDER

OF ALL THE

ABYSSAL BOOKS AND DOCTRINES

THIS BOOK BELONGS TO

INTRODUCTION

The Left-Hand Path of *Aphotism* paves a route for occultists to worship the void – our cosmic mother, wherefrom *all* life and magic is birthed into reality, and all matter returns upon its inescapable demise.

She is the grand arbiter of existence – the sculptor whose fair and starry hands have shaped the breath of time, darkness, and space into a dreamscape that hosts all possibilities and the infinitude of creation.

If not for the nanosecond in which she flashed into existence like divine lightning, reality itself would not be – time would have perished upon first light, and the phantasm of space would be a kingdom of *nothingness*. The withered husks of space and time would be little more than a memento of what *could* have been, yet never was – a liminal memory, lost within the cold, ever-expanding deeps of oblivion.

The void is our eldritch caretaker – the Acheronian cradle from which we arose, covered in the ash and star-soot of our primordial Armageddon. She is the garden from which humankind blossoms, cloaked in the gossamer chill and shadows of her kingdom.

She is our home and hearth – the asylum that offers transcendental power to *every* Aphotist who revels in her eclipse. Those that espouse the monarchy of the void shall feast upon the ambrosial fruits of her kingdom – *remarkable* blessings and bounties the likes of which few souls have *ever* beheld. These blessings, however, shall **only** be consumed by the worthy – by those who walk the Left-Hand Path of Aphotism and observe the sovereignty of the void.

With *The Abyssal Bible,* I aim to not only establish the Left-Hand Path of Aphotism but illustrate how it may be incorporated into one's everyday life and preexisting practices. This path was designed to be one of the most flexible occult arts available on the Left-Hand Path, offering its practitioners freedom in deciding their boundaries and malleability in the way they choose to bring Aphotism into their lives.

As you read *The Abyssal Bible,* I believe the power of Aphotism shall become *blindingly* apparent – a hybrid occult art that celebrates the all-permeating divinity of the void in an existentially glorious way that may be expressed spiritually, philosophically, or somewhere in the middle of these two methods.

I believe that *any* good occultist should be mindful of the void and appreciative of the fact that no god, religion, or reality as we know it would exist if not for her benevolence. While it is not mandatory that the occultist worships the void, they should *always* show their gratitude when discussing her, and they must never take for granted the reality she created.

THE FOUR PILLARS

I have quartered the contents of *The Abyssal Bible* into four internal books, each one exploring a core pillar of Aphotism's beliefs: essential information, ritual etiquette and holidays, our philosophies, and prewritten prayers of worship for our practitioners.

The *Book of Atoms* introduces Aphotism's central beliefs and philosophies – why and how we praise the void, the tenets and sins of Aphotism, and what our beliefs are regarding spirits, devils, and deities.

The *Book of Constellations* offers the reader a look at Aphotism's spiritual customs – our celebrations, days and events of power, ritual etiquette, and how we supplement our studies with ancient occult arts.

The *Book of Tides* explores the core philosophical beliefs of Aphotism – extraterrestrial life, spiritual dimensions, life after death, *endless* universes, and the true nature of the void as our preeminent deity.

The *Book of Echoes* offers the reader a collection of original, one-of-a-kind prayers – ready-to-recite rites of worship for everyday use, quick rituals, or even the affirmation of one's faith as an Aphotist.

Due to the wide breadth of information offered by *The Abyssal Bible,* the quartering of information is necessary to avoid confusing or overwhelming our readers. By keeping each key topic in a designated area of the book, it allows the reader to better focus on the topic at hand and absorb what is being read.

THE FIRST BOOK OF APHOTISM

CALLED THE

BOOK OF ATOMS

Within the Book of Atoms, you shall find a wealth of practical and foundational information — tenets, sins, introductory beliefs, and what it means to call yourself a devout apostle of the void – an Aphotist.

This first pillar of The Abyssal Bible will teach you everything you need to know to decide if this path is right for you – if its principles align with yours, and if you believe it can offer the power you seek.

A COSMIC FAITH

The Left-Hand Path of Aphotism is a complex yet intuitive and *powerful* hybridization of occultism, demonology, spiritual philosophy, and theoretical science – a *remarkably* malleable system of belief that celebrates the void and the exploration of her cosmic web in the pursuit of transcendental power.

The path of Aphotism is most accurately described as being a faith-philosophy – a study whose nature and malleability permit plasticity in how occultists interpret its belief systems, apply its teachings, and reap power from its practices. This dualistic nature of Aphotism allows occultists on both sides of the Left-Hand Path – theistic or atheistic – to bend and alter the ideas of Aphotism to fit their core beliefs without sacrificing said beliefs to religious dogma.

It is through this plastic nature of Aphotism that its teachings may supplement and cohabitate with the overarching religion or beliefs of an occultist – the path of Aphotism does **not** demand singular fealty, like many religions do. The void is the architect of all creation – without her, *every* faith, philosophy, kingdom, system, dogma, and idea would cease to exist, because existence itself would cease to exist. It is this all-permeating and tethering nature of the void that allows the occultist to celebrate her reign without spoiling their Left-Hand Path allegiances.

What does it mean to worship the void? Well, as detailed earlier, the Left-Hand Path of Aphotism is *extremely* malleable in nature, and what "worship" means will vary significantly from one Aphotist to the next. That said, as the founder of Aphotism, *my* version of worship entails teaching other occultists about the eldritch nature of the void, and exploring her star-wrought deeps in search of ancient power. As well, I maintain a constant degree of existential focus on the finite-yet-infinite nature of existence, savoring every breath that I borrow from the void.

As well as the void herself, Aphotists celebrate the *inconceivable* wealth of arcane knowledge that for eons has languished in the blackest reaches of time and space, waiting to be discovered by an occultist that understands the machinations of the void. Lost gods, and forgotten kingdoms; planes, worlds, and dimensions that lurk beyond the nebulous edge of our observable universe. As Aphotists, we believe the void will be the final dominion for occultists to explore – when every earthly system, religion, and mystery has been discovered, and ruins are all that remains of mankind's pious attempt at divinity, the void will still be rich with secrets, knowledge, and *unplumbed* depths of power waiting to be charted.

The void is the star-primed canvas upon which all of creation is afforded the privilege to exist – every world, galaxy, universe, religion, and god that has or will ever exist will **only** exist through the mercy of the void. She is the primeval creator of creators, whose strange and starry stage is merely *rented* by the gods, demons, and deities that dwell within her celestial sea. If, for some reason, the void were to collapse in on herself and cease to exist, she would take with her the crowns, memories, and kingdoms of every god that her cradle once birthed – Heaven and Hell, God, and the Devil – reduced to a feeble gasp of atoms in the cold, black sea of nothingness.

A power *this* intense – this immutable, and beyond even the ability of gods to escape – is a reality that *every* person should consider with reverence, awe, and a modicum of fear. On the Left-Hand Path of Aphotism, we believe that this divine power of the void should be *celebrated* – praised, and embraced as not only a necessary aspect of our existence, but an unparalleled catalyst for transcendental growth in our everyday lives and upon the Left-Hand Path.

Those that follow the Left-Hand Path of Aphotism shall explore the most *inconceivable* depths of the void, whose unplumbed nexuses of power have for eons been dredged only by gods. If the Aphotist is devoted to their worship of the void, they will reap profound blessings in life and upon the Left-Hand Path – those that extend *far* beyond the flesh, and beyond the feeble boundaries of this mortal realm.

On the Left-Hand Path of Aphotism, the blessings of the void will be offered in abundance to *all* that celebrate her primordial monarchy – knowledge of the abyss, and what strange powers lurk within her constellated deeps. Clarity of mind, and the purity of a spirit that has been illuminated by the divinest source – she who bore into being *every* atom, star, planet, breath, god, and glint of creation – the void, our caretaker – the Acheronian saint of Aphotism.

OF SEAS & STARS

On the Left-Hand Path of Aphotism, second to our worship of the void, occultists celebrate the oceans of our world – they, whose cold, mysterious depths share *countless* similarities with the void. Scarcely charted, and only superficially explored by a small handful of curious souls. Inhospitable, cryptic, and *teeming* with the secrets of perished eons – secrets that have long been buried beneath the black tides of our Earth's abyss, unbeheld yet by mortal eyes.

The oceans of our world are widely considered the most mystery-riddled, enigmatic places left for us to explore, surpassed only by the void. The oceans of Earth are a universe unto themselves – lightless, deep, and *brimming* with all manner of strange and aberrant forms – some alive, others dead, and still others tethered to the void. The same could be said for the oceans of *any* planet – they are a terrestrial, tangible reflection of the extraterrestrial, eternally gazing towards the void like a mirror whose murky panes vow to forever conceal her secrets. As one delves deeper into an ocean, they will bear witness to stranger and stranger sights – and, as one delves deeper into the void, the more bizarre, cryptic, and puzzling one will realize the nature of reality to be.

It is due to this shared, strange nature that the Left-Hand Path of Aphotism observes the oceans of our world in tandem with the void – they are both cut from the same ancient cloth, and as Aphotists gaze towards the stars in search of power, we *also* look towards the oceans as a physical representation of our religion and an extension of the void on Earth.

The oceans of Earth are divided into three primary zones – the *euphotic*, *dysphotic*, and *aphotic*. From there, these three zones are further subdivided into secondary zones that chart the descending scale of the ocean's ecology – smaller yet more abundantly available lifeforms dwell closer to the surface, and larger, stranger, more anomalous lifeforms inhabit the deeper reaches. As I am sure you have guessed, the aphotic zone of the ocean is where Aphotism's name takes inspiration – our religion celebrates the void and uses the deep sea as a symbol to represent the cold, tenebrous depths of space, where ancient secrets lie entombed beneath the sediment of time.

While Aphotists believe the oceans of Earth are an exemplary parallel to the void, we *also* believe the opposite to be true – that if one delves deep enough into the void, they shall behold sights and secreted truths of reality that defy comprehension, just like one would if they ventured to the deepest, blackest parts of our oceans. Lifeforms so aberrant that they resemble more the work of science fiction than any terrestrial creature – translucent, tentacled, barbed, bioluminescent, and rimed in the ageless shadows of eons. The lifeforms that are found in the darkest depths of our oceans have evolved in these unusual ways because **that** is what nature demanded – that is what was *necessary* for them to not only survive, but thrive amidst hostile conditions and impossible odds. I believe, as well, that this will be proven the case for many of the lifeforms that humanity shall eventually uncover in the furthest, oldest depths of the void – lifeforms that, according to our earthly logic and understanding, should not exist – *but do*.

On the Left-Hand Path of Aphotism, we regard the oceans as a *significant* source of spiritual strength, symbolism, and solace – since we cannot reach out and touch the void, the ocean is a way that we may physically look at and interact with an incarnation of our faith on Earth. I suppose it could be likened to the way a Catholic views a church or a Satanist does their altar – the ocean is a sort of sanctuary or temple for those that follow the path of Aphotism.

THE FIRST CHAPTER

CALLED

THE ABYSSAL TENETS

The Abyssal Tenets are three principles that we, as practitioners of Aphotism, adhere to – they are the guiding ethics that we abide by in life and upon the Left-Hand Path, never forgoing the direction they offer nor defying the standards that they represent.

The three tenets of Aphotism will guide, empower, clarify, and strengthen the Aphotist in *all* that they do – in life, and upon the Left-Hand Path. If these tenets are fully embraced and embodied, they shall reshape and realign the journey of the practitioner towards *unimaginable* fruits of knowledge, power, and transcendental illumination gifted by the void.

THE FIRST TENET

CALLED

KNOWLEDGE

On the Left-Hand Path of Aphotism, we believe no pursuit is greater than that of *knowledge* – to us, it is the seed of godliness. To possess knowledge, in either its earthly or transcendental form, is to hold the purest crux of power in one's hands – a plastic, malleable clay of *unlimited* potential, waiting to be reshaped into any number of limitless possibilities that may augment, guide, and empower one's life.

With sufficient knowledge at one's disposal, there is **nothing** beyond one's ability to attain, create, or tear into existence – knowledge is the catalyst that eclipses all other catalysts, offering *every* Aphotist the ability to reshape and redefine their journey in life and upon the Left-Hand Path with meticulous, intentional design. If the Aphotist does not possess sufficient knowledge, they do not possess the tools required to direct the current of their fate or future.

On the eldritch path of Aphotism, we believe that if a person is unwilling to pursue the attainment of knowledge, they are not only undeserving of a rich and powerful future, but *incapable* of manifesting it – the pursuit of knowledge in both its earthly and transcendental forms is the pursuit of a rewarding, well-lived life, so to forgo said pursuit is to forsake one's future, fate, and potential. As well, since the evolution and betterment of our world *depends* on those who are willing to pursue knowledge and do something significant with it, to decline the pursuit of knowledge is to forgo the positive contributions one might otherwise have contributed to the world.

THE SECOND TENET

CALLED

SOVEREIGNTY

On the Left-Hand Path of Aphotism, alongside the pursuit of knowledge, safeguarding one's sense of *sovereignty* is demanded of practitioners – without an iron grasp on one's autonomy, the Aphotist will never reach any remarkable depth of power. If the Aphotist does not have control over their mind and body, it is naïve to believe they possess the ability to notably affect or alter the unfolding of their fate.

If one does not have control over themselves, they do not have the ability to affect their destiny in any positive way – they shall watch, *helplessly*, as their life, path, and future are warped and redesigned by others – by those that have *actually* protected their autonomy. If the Aphotist desires an abundant life, transcendental power, or the blessings of the void, they *must* safeguard their sovereignty – they must preserve its ethereal flame, lest it be extinguished.

Though we cannot *fully* control what strange webs of fate the void shall weave for us, our sovereignty allows us to at least influence the weird ways they might unfold – our actions, no matter how minute, push the ripples of time in new directions. This, in turn, alters how our futures unfold – the seemingly minuscule leading to permanent alterations in how our fates are shaped. If the Aphotist's grip on their sovereignty is weak, so, *too*, will be their ability to augment and guide the unfurling of their life's web in a conscious way that leads to growth and power.

THE THIRD TENET

CALLED

SYMBIOSIS

On the Left-Hand Path of Aphotism, we strive for *symbiosis* with the void – a seamless, harmonious connection that may guide the worshipful Aphotist to *unfathomable* nexuses of transcendental power, knowledge, and primeval divinity. We, as apostles of the void, cherish our connection with her above all else – she is our source of comfort, clarity, and strength, and without her, we would have no faith.

No matter what, the Aphotist must *always* attempt to foster, maintain, and nurture their connection to the void – without her guidance, the Aphotist shall find themselves lost upon this Left-Hand Path. The polestar of Aphotism is the grace of the void, so to neglect one's union with her is akin to quenching one's lone source of light amidst a cold, caliginous night – the Aphotist *must* ensure that their tether to the void is nourished, healthy, and free of tangles.

If the Aphotist does not nurture their connection to the void, they *will* lose it – and if an Aphotist loses their connection to the void, they have, *essentially*, become useless – like a toothless shark, or an angel whose wings have been pinioned. The Aphotist, in their pursuit of illumination via the blessings of the void, *must* uphold their connection to her the same as they would with any spirit, god, demon, or thing of power. The greater the Aphotist's connection is to the void, the more potent the blessings they shall receive – your benedictions will reflect your effort, so it would prove wise to nurture your relationship.

THE THIRD CHAPTER

CALLED

THE ABYSSAL SINS

The Abyssal Sins are three of the most disgraceful, self-sabotaging, and sacrilegious behaviors that an Aphotist could err to engage in – and they *must* be passionately avoided, lest the Aphotist unwittingly causes irreparable damage to their pursuits – both in life and upon the constellated path of Aphotism.

The three sins of Aphotism, if not heeded, shall be the unmaking of the Aphotist – these three sins are the most common, self-sown downfalls of not only Aphotists but *all* occultists, as well as the average, orthodox human being. These three sins are found everywhere in our society, poisoning the potential, perceptions, and power of every soul that partakes in their subterfuge – unaware that these habits they embrace are, *in reality*, weakening their spirit and slating their days ahead for frailty, and mediocrity.

THE FIRST SIN

CALLED

IGNORANCE

If the Aphotist hopes to attain knowledge from the void, their mind must not be clouded by the murky fog of *ignorance* – that proud, dull haze that makes fools believe themselves to be kings and the naïve to be prophets. Who can learn – who can be taught and guided if they believe that nothing remains for them to learn – if they believe that they are a gilded paragon of wisdom, too wise to become a student?

The Aphotist does not commit the sin of ignorance simply by not knowing something – that would be contrary to human nature. The truth is that nobody knows or understands *anything*, until they do – that is what learning is. No, the sinfulness of ignorance lies in one's *unwillingness* to learn – to go through that journey of discovery and perceiving oneself as a student rather than a master – because *that* is the only way that one may truly uncover the unknown.

On the Left-Hand Path of Aphotism, we believe in committing ourselves to the everlasting pursuit of transformation – forever eager to study, learn, and embrace whatever change is necessary to not only become a better occultist, but a more insightful and intelligent human being. There can be no profound growth in life or upon the Left-Hand Path until one has made their mind receptive, and open – like the seed cannot blossom and grow into a fruit-bearing tree until it has been sown, watered, and nourished.

THE SECOND SIN

CALLED

SERVITUDE

If the Aphotist seeks sovereignty and autonomous rule in life and upon the Left-Hand Path, they must avoid succumbing to *servitude* – the oppressing of one's soul by another being, ideology, religion, or system. The faith of Aphotism *demands* that one's sovereignty is upheld – if the practitioner does not preserve their autonomy, they are unfit to possess any notable measure of transcendental knowledge.

The servile occultist is a *useless* occultist – nothing more than an oxymoron or a poorly crafted façade of the real thing. A *true* occultist could never allow themselves to become servile – to be commanded, manipulated, or contorted to satisfy the will of *any* earthly or unearthly force. Servility defies the very nature of what it means to be an occultist, and what it means to follow the Left-Hand Path – servitude will *never* lead to transcendental power or growth.

The blessing of transcendentality is a *privilege*, not a right – it does not belong to beggars, the weak of constitution, or those who are willing to forfeit the sovereignty of their soul. Transcendental power is the honor of kings, conquerors, sages, and those of *unyielding* constitution – the dedicated student, the educative master, and those souls that have proven themselves worthy of beholding the divine. On the Left-Hand Path of Aphotism, we believe that only those who uphold their autonomy deserve to enjoy the blessings of the void – the timeless knowledge of realms, worlds, and universes beyond our own and what old powers lie buried within their depths.

THE THIRD SIN

CALLED

DISHARMONY

If the Aphotist seeks the blessings of the void, they must avoid letting *disharmony* sow its seed – there can be no communion with the void if the occultist allows their soul to have a dissonant bond with she whose liminal dreamscape we inhabit. Only those who nurture their connection to the void shall ever inherit her blessings, or bear witness to the power that she for *eons* has birthed, coveted, and hidden.

How can the occultist expect to attain the blessings of the void if they do not caretake their connection to her cosmos? As a seed requires fertile soil, rain, and a nurturing environment in order to bloom and bear fruit, so, too, must the Aphotist caretake their covenant with the void if they hope to ever inherit the bounties she may provide – knowledge, power, and the secrets of lost eons that may shepherd one to deeper, constellated depths of transcendentality.

On the Left-Hand Path of Aphotism, we believe in honoring oneself through honoring the void – that, as sentient, physical manifestations of her aphotic reign, to denounce one's connection to the void is to offend one's cosmic origins. We each enjoy the *wondrous* gifts of life, intellect, and consciousness because of the void – if *she* did not exist, *we* would not exist, nor would anything else that humans oft take for granted. We, as Aphotists, pity those who deny and tarnish their nature as an extension of the void – those blind souls who meander through life with a warped perception of their place in creation.

THE FOURTH CHAPTER

CALLED

IN HER SHADOWS

On the Left-Hand Path of Aphotism, we believe in intelligent life beyond humanity – spirits, demons, ghosts, gods, and extraterrestrial life, *all* of which have for untold eons *flourished* within the strange, dark, and virtually unexplored byways of the void.

In Aphotism, we celebrate this idea that life exists *abundantly* within the void – as well, we believe it is time that the world stops considering this notion the sole domain of science fiction. To be confident that intelligent life exists beyond humanity is not a matter of ignorance but evidence of a logical mind, and when considering the endlessness of the void, it is almost *guaranteed* that we are far from alone.

THE ETERNALITY OF SPIRITS

On the star-lined path of Aphotism, we believe that *every* person possesses an inextinguishable ember of life that can never *truly* experience the dreaded phenomenon of death – at least, not in the clinical, cold, and permanent manner that most people tend to imagine when they think of dying. This eternal essence within you – call it a soul, consciousness, energy, or whatever you prefer – we, as Aphotists, believe that this phantasm of light is *imperishable*.

This soul of yours – this primordial star that burns within you and gives life to the blood, bone, flesh, and sinew of your earthly being – is a fragment of the void left behind from the moment she first gave assent to your creation. Like a piece taken from the most intricate puzzle, to be returned to help restore the greater picture upon one's demise, the soul can *never* die, for it is an expression of the void herself.

When, at last, the hour comes when you must die, and the final breath is wrung from your lungs, your soul shall leave your body – rigor mortis will claim your once-spirited, loud, joyous, and earthly husk, and the last skinny rays of light that meet your eyes shall fade to black. Darkness, then, shall envelope you – or, at least, whatever remains of the concept that you regard as "you." As before you were last born, you shall return to the liminal dreamscape of nothingness that birthed you – and, somehow, you *will* remember that nothingness. It will be familiar, though its familiarity *should* be impossible since it is devoid of any matter, life, or identifiable stimuli that one can associate with past senses, wherefrom that feeling of familiarity arises. Yet, it will *still* be familiar – it will still feel as if you have spent your whole past life searching for this place, and that is because you will have returned home – *to the void.*

On the nebulous path of Aphotism, we believe that when one's body dies, their soul returns to the void and begins the process of rebirth in a world, realm, plane, universe, or dimension that best mirrors the core attachments it made during its past life – *this* is how a religion practiced in life may forever alter the course of one's soul upon death, guiding it to specific realms such as Heaven or Hell. Your soul is the sum of *every* action, decision, belief, feeling, and desire that has culminated over the duration of your *countless* incarnations, each one affecting the way your next life unfolds – be careful of what you do with your soul, because it shall never leave you.

With this notion in mind of your soul being forever reincarnated within the cold, eldritch depths of the void, Aphotists believe that *every* realm where the soul may be reborn can be interacted with, at will, by those who possess a sufficient understanding of either strange sciences or the occult. As I described previously, the soul may be reborn in any number of realms, planes, universes, or dimensions, or on any world found within these places – but this does **not** mean the physics, properties, or limitations of these places are equal. A planet is far different than a universe, or a dimension – where you must travel to another planet in order to feel its soil or interact with its lifeforms, spaces like dimensions exist all around you at this very second – most of which are imperceptible, and incapable of being gazed upon by human eye or perceived by our limited intellect.

That is what we believe happens to the human soul upon death, and why the paranormal exists – when the body dies and its soul returns to the void, that soul goes to a new dimension until it is ready to be reborn elsewhere. The dimension of the soul is one that overlaps ours, allowing the spirits of that plane to observe and interact with *us* freely, though not necessarily the other way around – this is because the soul would be considered a higher dimensional entity, and we cannot perceive a fourth dimension.

Think about geometry, for a moment – if you look at a flat, two-dimensional drawing of a square, you cannot see the faces that would transform it into a three-dimensional cube – to you, it is just a square. Thankfully, we are able to perceive life with three dimensions – this is what allows you to understand and turn a square into a cube. Now, try to imagine a four-dimensional evolution of a cube – better yet, try to draw, paint, or sculpt one. See how difficult of a time you have, and if it does not make you feel like your mind is imploding. The four-dimensional evolution of a cube is called a *tesseract* – there are theoretical models made of what a tesseract would look like, but absolutely no examples of a tesseract can be observed, *by us,* in life on Earth or amongst the void – and that is because we cannot perceive the fourth dimension as three-dimensional beings.

As Aphotists, we believe that the plane of the spirit contains an *unfathomable* wealth of knowledge for those able to interact with it – be it through science or the occult, it makes little difference, for they are two halves of the same existential coin – and if you venture far enough into one, you shall, *eventually*, encounter the other. I believe that, with a sufficient caliber of science, the existence of spirits, demons, rebirth, Heaven, Hell, and *all* other religious topics can be proven or disproven – even if we can never *directly* perceive them and must, therefore, create a technology that allows us to bend and bypass the boundaries set for us as three-dimensional entities.

I believe that the occult is an *exceptional* vessel for one to use in their exploration of not only the void, but the realms, planes, and dimensions of spirits. I *also* believe that the Left-Hand Path of Aphotism is one of the most compelling, dynamic, and potent occult arts for this endeavor because *that* is how I designed it – to serve as an unparalleled device for scouring the stars in search of knowledge through the bifocaled lens of faith and science, neither one silencing the other in the name of dogmatic virtue, nor sacrificing the pursuit of truth for the fanatical fruits of piety. As an Aphotist, you should embrace the pursuits of *both* the truth and transcendentality, for they are equal in importance – a blind king may still be a king, but if he cannot see the kingdom he has built, what good is the grandeur of his crown?

IN THE COMPANY OF DEVILS

At the abyssal core of Aphotism lies the ancient art of *demonology* – the study of demons, their nature, and the ways they may offer transcendental power and knowledge to occultists judged worthy. On the nebulous path of Aphotism, the study of demons is second to our worship of and communion with the void – it is a fundamental aspect of our beliefs, and if one intends to regard themselves as an Aphotist, they *must* have at least a cursory understanding of and interest in the blasphemous art of the demonic.

This is not to say that the Aphotist must *believe* in demons or perform rituals against their will – there is no obligation to sacrifice one's ideals, beliefs, or boundaries in the name of Aphotism. That said, the Aphotist *is* expected to build a foundational wealth of demonological knowledge – learning about how this art is incorporated into the whole of Aphotism, and in what ways our doctrines use demonology to explain and enhance our core beliefs, philosophy, and concepts. As well, it is vital for the Aphotist to be proficient in demonology so that they can better appreciate the metaphors, symbolism, and nuances utilized in Aphotism that might only be noticed by the sightful – by those who know what to look for, where to look, and how to interpret what they find.

Though demonology is an ancient study, there are *countless* ways to explore this long-reviled avenue of the Left-Hand Path – most of which, to this day, are still waiting to be discovered by those who dare explore the uncharted, unlit corridors of the occult. When we think of demonology, we typically think of the spirits that belong to the infamous hierarchy of the *Ars Goetia* – Ipos, Stolas, Murmur, Paimon, Bael, and so forth. Modern demonologists are very limited in the scope of demonic spirits they know of and are engaged with – and even *further* limited in how they conceive the very nature and existence of these spirits – as *purely* spiritual entities, usually bound to the kingdom of Hell as a solitary, one-off result of Christianity, Heaven, and the rule of God.

On the celestial path of Aphotism, there are many practitioners that integrate the Goetia demons into their studies – or, perhaps it is more accurate to say that many Goetic occultists find the unconstrained and existential ideas of Aphotism *alluring*, leading them to mix Aphotism into the coagulated, diverse mélange that is their occult studies. Whichever the case may be, Aphotism encourages the exploration of the Goetia hierarchy, if that is what the Aphotist wishes to do – but, if inclined to pursue the Goetia hierarchy in one's studies, it is encouraged that the Aphotist seeks out *additional* demonic hierarchies. That said, Aphotism's beliefs regarding the nature and inclusion of demons in one's studies are rather unique, and unlikely to mingle perfectly with more archaic or traditional views of the Left-Hand Path.

One of the more unique beliefs of Aphotism is that demonic spirits, like human souls, exist elsewhere in a **physical** form – perhaps in a dimension that is *far* higher than the paltry, three-dimensional plane we call home. Depending on how many universes, realms, and dimensions exist, this could *infinitely* be the case – endless hierarchies of demonic spirits thriving in endless realms that exceed the limits of our meager, three-dimensional plane, born of flesh and blood like you and I, yet are imperceptible and therefore deemed ethereal beings. With this notion in mind, the idea of limiting oneself to exploring a single hierarchy of demons is *absurd,* when there may be *countless* others waiting to be unveiled by perceptive, assiduous occultists – by those who are dissatisfied with being limited to the resources that were founded hundreds or *thousands* of years ago.

On the Left-Hand Path of Aphotism, practitioners endeavor to unlock new bastions of demonological knowledge through the exploration and worship of the void – scouring her black tides of stars that the seminal occultists of ages passed once plumbed in search of the knowledge that you and I now regard as routine, but in their time was *revolutionary*. One of the overarching pursuits of Aphotism is to, like our occult forefathers, reveal the unknown for both the illumination of our apostles and the Left-Hand Path as a whole – and, in this pursuit, we must look primarily towards the greater realm of the demonic within the void for an opportunity to discover new, *exhilarating* wealths of transcendental knowledge that shall not only empower occultists, but *inspire*

them to reignite the torch of our predecessors and carry it eagerly into the abyssal depths of the void.

As apostles of Aphotism, our appetite for demonic knowledge extends *beyond* the readily known and accepted boundaries set for us by the occultists of centuries past – boundaries defined not by tyranny, censorship, or piety, but by a lull in innovation and a dearth of new discoveries. You see, the limits of humanity's development in *any* field, art, or study are demarcated by our most recent advances – the greatest achievements become the benchmark that the next generation of explorers must either shrink into the shadows of or attempt to surpass. Once the great occultists of yore were dead, and our puerile world began tasting the cold, industrial fruits of the modern age, society's interest in magic, occultism, and demonology dwindled to a historic low – this, largely due to our misguided belief that the realms of spirits and demons are primitive stigma left over from our archaic past that we must outgrow, as we fine-tune and polish our image as a scientific race.

Though humanity in ages past commonly misused the spiritual to explain what we now understand as ordinary acts and feats of science, you cannot fault an uneducated populace for having less knowledge than you – to use the supernatural in an attempt to explain the unexplained was a standard practice up until the mid-to-late 1700s. The misguided beliefs of our ancestors and their misattribution of science to the supernatural does **not** mean the supernatural does not exist – the word *supernatural* itself refers to something beyond our understanding that is not **yet** proven by science. At one point in time, it was not yet scientifically proven that we orbit the Sun, that the Earth is spherical, or that black holes exist. One of the overarching beliefs of Aphotism is that, much like the curvature of Earth and the existence of black holes, it will someday not only be proven that the soul exists, but higher-dimensional entities that we would regard, visually and behaviorally, as *demonic* – horrors in some currently-unnamed and uncharted corridor of space, lurking on the dimly-lit outskirts of our universe or in one *unfathomably* far away from ours – yet within immediate reach, by their will and discretion, at a moment's notice.

THE HORRORS OF INFINITUDE

On the ethereal path of Aphotism, there are spirits, demons, and *horrors* – aberrations without names, grafted together from shadows and stars into every shape both conceivable and forbidden to behold by our nescient minds. These horrors – these *hideous,* patchwork mockeries of life that traverse with ease the gossamer veil that separates the physical from the spiritual – they, if found and uncovered by the occultist, may offer an *unfathomable* wellspring of power the likes of which few souls have ever seen.

These amorphous colossi of the void are the living vestiges of her primeval birth – vulgar, *undulating* goliaths of raw power, patched together without a plan or design into what the human eye could only perceive as *nightmarish*. But, these entities – these dreadful constructs of the void – they have beheld sights and wonders that would *paralyze* our fragile mortal minds – things that would forever alter our perception of life, death, and what occurs in those unlit places between the stars, where light itself is afraid to cast its rays, and few occultists have ever endeavored to chart their cold, mysterious depths.

When we discuss intelligent life *beyond* humanity, whether it be alien life out in the cosmos or entities from the spiritual realms, we typically assume that such life will resemble us – bipedal, with two eyes, a mouth, limbs, and anatomy that we could look at and confidently say, "*that* is alive." I find this view to be unforgivably ignorant, absent of both realism and imagination – compare the diversity of life on Earth for proof: a cat to an octopus, an alligator to a wasp, a human to a shark. The life on our meager little planet is so *wildly* diverse, with each species sharing barely any similarities to the next – so who are we, the lowly human race, to suggest that in the endlessness of space and across potentially *infinite* universes, that all, most, or even *any* intelligent life we may unveil would resemble us in the slightest?

It is our arrogant and self-aggrandizing nature as a species that compels us to believe that any form of intelligent life that we could one day discover *must* meet the vapid criteria of *looking* human. We have even gone so far as to depict our angels, devils, and gods as being human in their appearance – deified, omnipotent caricatures of ourselves for the masses to either fear or adulate. Though it is true that *some* spirits and entities might have humanoid attributes and characteristics, this should be thought of as the exception, not a rule – *especially* when it comes to the Left-Hand Path and the entities that one might encounter in their pursuit of transcendental power.

If the Aphotist wishes to explore the oft-tenebrous, strange corridors of the Left-Hand Path, they must be comfortable with and ready to encounter a wide variety of entities – *most* of which will not fit into the rigid physical parameters that society has come to expect from spiritual entities. The vast majority of entities that one might encounter in these murky byways of the Left-Hand Path will undoubtedly be a shock to one's senses – hideous creatures of ether and wild magic, cobbled together into some of the strangest forms imaginable – and many that are *far* too bizarre for our fragile minds to envision. These entities roam the star-paved backroads of creation, waiting to be revealed by those souls who not only know *where* to look for the knowledge they desire, but are not afraid to explore the shadows in which they have been buried since the beginning of time.

These ancient sentinels – these nightmarish colossi of the void have *always* been there, sailing through worlds, realms, universes, and the gossamer fabric of time itself, waiting to be unveiled by those souls brave enough to venture into the abyss in search of transcendental knowledge. As an Aphotist, *you* are one of these souls – an eager explorer of the void, devoted to the interminable pursuit of power, self-mastery, and illumination in life and upon the Left-Hand Path. In this endeavor, the horrors of the void shall prove to be an *excellent* wellspring of abyssal power that shall galvanize your studies – assuming that you are able to unveil these entities, of course.

In most avenues of the Left-Hand Path, if you wish to communicate with spiritual entities, the process is *fairly* straightforward – there are names, dates of power, offerings, sigils, orisons, grimoires, and all manner of timeworn tools at your disposal that will not only help you understand the nature of a given spirit, but call upon them with virtuosic precision. An example of spirits that are typically easy to call upon and who have a wealth of accessible tools for doing so would be the demons of the infamous *Ars Goetia* hierarchy. The 72 infernal spirits that make up this prestigious hierarchy have been *extensively* written about, studied, and recorded for centuries, and there are now *countless* texts that are available for occultists to learn anything and everything they desire about these spirits – unfortunately, the same cannot be said yet about the horrors of the void.

At the time of writing *The Abyssal Bible*, I cannot think of a single noteworthy book or occultist that has attempted to not only discuss these entities, but explore and demystify their nature, origins, names, and details relevant to invocation for the benefit of the Left-Hand Path. The argument could be made, though, that this upsetting dearth of information is the very thing that makes these entities so alluring, and worth pursuing – they are an uncharted source of transcendental power, known by few and beheld by even fewer. This lack of accessible information surrounding the horrors of the void is the aspect of their existence that we are *most* beguiled by – that which distresses us is that which fascinates us, and compels us to explore further in search of answers.

Though it is impossible to *completely* separate the unknown from that which *thrives* on the unknown, the Left-Hand Path of Aphotism offers occultists a wide variety of tools, methods, and principles that can ease one's ability to commune with the horrors of the void – to establish lines of communication, converse successfully, and amass information that will prove necessary to call upon the same entities, again, in the future – names, histories, hierarchies, summoning elements, and the types of information that one may use to call upon well-known entities, such as the 72 demons of the Goetic hierarchy. The tools that Aphotism provides allow the occultist to venture further into the realm of the unknown than their preexisting toolkit may have permitted – and, in one's exploration of new frontiers of the occult, these Abyssian tools will prove to be irreplaceable.

THE SECOND BOOK OF APHOTISM

CALLED THE

BOOK OF CONSTELLATIONS

The Book of Constellations offers you a wealth of information regarding Aphotism's spiritual beliefs and customs – our holidays, events of power, and how we perform rituals in celebration of the void.

This second pillar of The Abyssal Bible will reveal to you the ways in which we exercise our faith and find power through the void – this book will prove vital in deciding how you should pursue Aphotism.

THE FIRST CHAPTER

CALLED

ETIQUETTE & PRACTICE

To consort with spirits deserves a certain degree of refinement from the occultist – etiquette, dexterity, and gratitude that we, as Aphotists, are expected to *always* uphold. Our ability to call upon and nurture meaningful connections to spirits is a gift that *must* be respected – it is not a guarantee nor a given, and it must *never* be taken for granted by the Aphotist.

This chapter of *The Abyssal Bible* will explore our guidelines for ethically and sustainably consorting with spirits – performing rituals, creating an altar, interacting with spirits, and establishing a lifelong, mutually beneficial relationship with these spirits.

RITUALS

As with any art upon the Left-Hand Path, the faith-philosophy of Aphotism utilizes *rituals* as a means of not only galvanizing and inspiring disciples, but leading them to the transcendental blessings of the void – knowledge, power, and the primeval secrets of our universe that for many cold, bleak millennia have been buried amongst the stars, unbeheld even by the wisest occultists of Earth's present and past.

Through the incorporation of rituals in one's study of Aphotism, the occultist may ascend unthinkable heights of transcendentality the likes of which few occultists have ever summited – those that for eons have towered *far* beyond sight and grasp, deep into the Acheronian abyss that surrounds this hellscape droplet of light that we so affectionately call Earth.

The ritual etiquette of Aphotism reflects what you would expect to find in any other avenue upon the Left-Hand Path, though with a few caveats – while most Aphotists *do* perform rituals, these rituals are unlike typical occult rituals, in many ways. One of the more differentiating aspects of an aphotic ritual is that many of said rituals are directed towards the void, rather than an individual entity, like a demon. The void to Aphotists is akin to God as a Catholic, or the Devil to a Satanist – she is our divine North, towards whose starry dreamscape we pray, rejoice, and demonstrate our faithfulness to her dominion.

An Aphotist's ritual can either be partly or *entirely* performed in honor of the void – a brief expression of one's reverence before a larger ceremony, or the sole intention of the ritual in question – there is no "preferred" way for the Aphotist to celebrate their faith nor express their praise for the void. As is the objective of most rituals upon the Left-Hand Path, the purpose of a ritual is twofold – to express one's spiritual beliefs through artistic symbolism, and to open lines of communication with an entity not of this world in hopes that it may lead to an exchange of knowledge or power – sometimes, this entity is a spirit, and other times, it may be the void herself.

On the Left-Hand Path of Aphotism, we celebrate the void through our rituals as a means of showing our allegiance to her monarchy – these rituals may be performed in any way, at any time, and in any location the Aphotist deems fit, though we *always* encourage one to follow local laws and ordinances while *also* ensuring that one's actions do not cause senseless harm to oneself or any person or animal. Though I cannot speak on behalf of all Aphotists, our religion teaches and encourages its apostles to respect *every* expression of the void – the planets, oceans, stars, forests, wildlife, and everything else that one shares the divine atoms of known creation with – the oxygen, carbon, hydrogen, and nitrogen that unites all incarnations of our mother, the void.

ALTARS

As with most avenues of the Left-Hand Path, those who follow the constelled art of Aphotism often decide to construct and utilize an *altar* – a physical place of worship, assembled by and tailored to the unique needs and comforts of the practitioner. The Aphotist's altar is a sacred place – it is where they shall perform most of their rituals, discover the lost secrets of eons past, and learn about themselves as they brave the gales of life and the Left-Hand Path.

To the Aphotist, there are few places on Earth that rival the comfort, peace, and security that they find in their altar – it is a refuge, a fortress, an academy, and an *endless* adventure wrapped into a fragment of the void that is 100% under their control. It is a canvas for their uncensored expression, blank until it is painted with the emotions, symbols, offerings, desires, and personality of the Aphotist – their altar is a sincere reflection of their values and ambitions upon the Left-Hand Path and in life as a whole.

The Aphotist's altar is an asylum – a sanctuary *far* removed from the vaudevillian chaos and theatrics of our dystopian world. At the altar, one shall find uninterrupted peace, direction, inspiration, and the comfort of the void, for the altar is one's corporeal window into her dreamscape. To an Aphotist, their altar is a liminal looking glass – an escape route to another time, place, and realm, where their soul is unfettered and free to pursue its ambitions without the fear of persecution, oppression, or stifling by a society that collectively suppresses the voices and desires of those that dare separate themselves from the blind and unconscious hivemind of the masses.

As a place of comfort and worship, the Aphotist's altar is oftentimes built in a location owned by the occultist – an attic, cellar, office, or bedroom are the most common locations where an altar may be constructed. The Aphotist's altar should be viewed as a sacred space, and as a sacred space, be created in a location that is comfortable to use and easy to access. If the Aphotist's altar is difficult to access or cumbersome, odds are high that it will be rarely used – and, if used at all, it will not be used as often or efficiently as possible. Your altar should *always* be constructed with peace and comfort in mind, for it is where you will spend a *tremendous* amount of time honing your craft as a celebrant of the void.

For some Aphotists, having one altar is simply not enough to satisfy their needs, and they may choose to assemble a *second* altar – this altar is oftentimes transportable, capable of being deconstructed and rebuilt with relative ease. This course of action is usually taken by occultists who wish to use an altar outdoors, surrounded and galvanized by the power and beauty of nature – *especially* the water and the void above, since these are the two most prevalent symbols that Aphotism references in its scriptures, prayers, and philosophy. To be closer to the water or to the stars will bring most Aphotists a profound sense of invigoration – a binding connection to the Earth, the cosmos, and to the occultist's innermost self, both during their rituals and once they return to the monotony and bedlam of their everyday life.

At the altar, you are *omnipotent* – you are god, and the universe. You are the shadows, and the storms;

the oceans and the stars. As an Aphotist, when you stand before your altar, *you* are the shaper of your destiny – the grand architect of your present, your future, and *every* potentiality that can, will, or does exist before you. The Aphotist's altar is a place of discovery and creation where the occultist may not only wash away the grime of life, but *meticulously* design the person they wish to become and the life they wish to live – and on the Left-Hand Path, you shall know no place of greater hearth and comfort than at the constellated steps of your abyssal altar.

SUMMONING ELEMENTS

In almost every faith, philosophy, and practice that can be found upon the Left-Hand Path, *summoning elements* are commonplace and have been used for centuries by occultists. A summoning element is a gift or tithe of sorts – a token of appreciation given by the occultist to a spirit or entity in exchange for said entity's blessings, benedictions, or assistance.

Every spirit, be it a demon, god, or some other type of metaphysical entity, possesses a unique array of preferred offerings that make them happy and may elicit their cooperation – no different than how you and I have our preferences, and how being offered something you enjoy may improve your mood and make you more likely to partake in a trade of effort or energy, which is *precisely* the goal of any ritual.

It may not always be easy to uncover the preferred summoning elements of a spirit – *especially* when the occultist is working with abyssal spirits, many of which have either not been documented or have very little information readily available about their preferences or personalities. That said, it is **always** better to add non-specific summoning elements to a ritual than to not include any at all – below is the list of summoning elements that we commonly use for the rituals, rites, and celebrations of Aphotism:

- o Incense and candles.
- o Shells, fossils, and bones.
- o Chalices, goblets, etc.
- o Gold, silver, etc.
- o Emeralds, rubies, etc.
- o Fresh water, sand, and clay.
- o Sigils, sacred markings, etc.
- o Herbs, flowers, etc.
- o Antiques, baubles, etc.
- o Alcohol.

A SAFE VOYAGE

As with any avenue of the Left-Hand Path, caution is advised when exploring the void or delving into the art of Aphotism. The nature of the occult is that of the unknown, enigmatic, and unexpected – and that is true for the *risks* as much as it is the rewards.

One of the primary pursuits of Aphotism is to look upon that which has not yet been beheld by mortal eyes – to consort with entities from worlds beyond one's wildest comprehension and attain from them the knowledge and power of unfathomable realms.

With this pursuit comes inherent risk for those that do not take caution with each step forward – those that are arrogant, impatient, or do not show respect for the entities with which they consort. For those who show due respect, patience, and a willingness to learn, however, few dangers should arise in their exploration of the void and her immortal kingdom.

THE SECOND CHAPTER

CALLED

CELEBRATIONS

On the Left-Hand Path of Aphotism, holidays and celebratory events are plentiful, *all* of which are an *extraordinary* opportunity for the Aphotist to reap power, refine their ritual efficiency, and embolden their beliefs as an unyielding celebrant of the void.

This chapter of *The Abyssal Bible* will explore the most significant and auspicious days in a calendar year, for the Aphotist – celebrations that not only highlight the intensity, beauty, and strength of the void but the Aphotist's home within her kingdom.

SOUL TITHE

The 10th day of every month.

On the tenth day of every month, Aphotists partake in rituals, prayers, and celebrations in observation of *Soul Tithe* – a day of deep reflection, tranquility, and the rekindling of one's connection to the void.

The numerical significance of this day will be seen by those familiar with the Pythagorean value of the number ten – regarded as the most sacred number, denoting the nine bodies of our solar system and a veiled, tenth body, referred to as "Counter–Earth."

LIGHT OF THE ATER

February 18th – 25th

During *Light of the Ater,* Aphotists celebrate their nature as living fragments of the void – revenants of the cosmos, born from her primordial darkness and blessed with the divine spark of consciousness with which we experience the phenomenon of life.

For this holiday, many Aphotists choose to partake in group celebrations – grand displays, parties, and hedonistic revelries are commonly held, allowing Aphotists to develop new kinships with others that recognize and revere our cosmic mother – *the void.*

THE APOSTLE'S DAY

April 11th

On *The Apostle's Day,* the Aphotist is encouraged to celebrate themselves and their journey upon the Left-Hand Path – their achievements, their growth as both a person and practitioner, and what things they hope to accomplish on the murky road ahead.

The majority of Aphotists choose to celebrate this holiday in solitude, focusing on private displays of worship, relaxation, and performing rituals that are oriented around self-empowerment and wellbeing.

THE APOSTLE'S NIGHT

May 22nd

The Apostle's Night is a celebration of the Aphotist and an opportunity for them to relax and reinspire their mind, body, and spirit – shedding the sorrows and misery of life, and getting themselves back on course if they have strayed from their desired path.

The name of this holiday is **not** a limitation of how or when the Aphotist may celebrate – "the night" is symbolic of the peace and tranquility that many occultists feel when the sun abandons her seraphic throne, and the moon reclaims the icebound night.

On this day, Aphotists are encouraged to celebrate however they see fit – some choose rituals, prayer, and feasts, while others might prefer to hike, draw, sleep in, or find another method of recharging their batteries, so to speak. So long as the Aphotist uses this time to slow down, refresh, and reexamine the path ahead, it should be a fruitful Apostle's Night.

TIDE HARVEST

August 2nd –11th

An event of *extraordinary* power, *Tide Harvest* is a nine-day-long celebration of the devils, horrors, and abyssal gods that the Aphotist turns to in their rituals, rites, and studies upon the Left-Hand Path.

A typical celebration of Tide Harvest will involve well-planned, intricate rituals, feasts, and seances, either enjoyed alone or with a close-knit group of likeminded occultists. Each festivity that is staged in observance of Tide Harvest should be devoted to *at least* one demon the Aphotist has found to be instrumental to their life, faith, or Left-Hand Path.

DEMON REVELS

July 1st | September 15th | December 24th

When *Demon Revels* rolls around, occultists of all paths and denominations celebrate the history and presence of devils on Earth – how they have aided humanity's development throughout the centuries, and how they continue to empower those amongst us that choose to study and preserve the old ways.

Over the centuries, this holiday has been observed in *countless* different ways by practitioners of the Left-Hand Path – from hedonistic parties or blood magic to self-possessions or a simple communion with nature. Today, occultists choose to celebrate Demon Revels with feasts, rituals, and alignments that honor the demonic spirits they have welcomed into their life and studies upon the Left-Hand Path.

HALLOWEEN

October 31ˢᵗ

There are few holidays of greater significance for occultists than *Halloween* – a sacred day of magic, revelry, and the embrace of traditions that *most* of our industrial world has long since abandoned. On this powerful day, even the most secular souls will undoubtedly find themselves drawn to the strange, the macabre, and that vaporous veil that separates our world from those of spirits, devils, and horrors.

On Halloween, Aphotists tend to celebrate with an unmatched enthusiasm – feasts, gatherings, group rituals, séances, and ornate displays of one's faith are common. Some practitioners, however, choose to spend Halloween in reflection – focusing on the solstice ahead, the coming new year, and the ways in which they would like to alter their path in life.

MARINER'S DAY

November 22nd

On *Mariner's Day,* Aphotists reflect on the storms they have weathered throughout the year – painful losses, adversities, conflicts, and disappointments. As well, the Aphotist attempts to make peace with and lay to rest what no longer is, so they can avoid bringing that pain and suffering into the new year.

In observance, many Aphotists will grieve, mourn, celebrate, or pray – performing rituals in honor of what they have weathered, in memory of what they have lost, and in remembrance of what once was but shall never be again. As well, it is common for Aphotists to host group feasts, rituals, and séances that bring together like-minded souls for a chance to bury their ghosts and set sail for a new horizon.

NEW TIDES

December 29th – 31st

The last *official* celebration of the year, *New Tides,* is a three-day-long observation of the year that has been lived and the new year that lies ahead – a year that is *filled* with opportunity, growth, and magic.

During New Tides, many Aphotists celebrate with small gatherings, intimate feasts, and group rituals that focus on boosting morale and fostering a sense of optimism amongst the revelers. As well, private prayers and rituals pertaining to health, happiness, and fortune are commonly performed by Aphotists as they steel their mind and spirit for the new year.

THE THIRD CHAPTER

CALLED

ABYSSAL EVENTS

On the Left-Hand Path of Aphotism, holidays are
not the only notable occurrences that occultists can
attain power from – natural events and phenomena
have proven to be just as potent in empowering the
Aphotist that *efficiently* channels the raw energy of
these grand events into their rituals or celebrations.

RAINSTORMS

One of the most *powerful* events for an Aphotist to experience is a *rainstorm* – a simple act of nature, but one that brings us peace, strength, and comfort.

To watch the skies roll black and weep down their cold, gloomy sheets of glass – to listen to the city's deafening chaos grind to a shivering halt – brings the Aphotist a *tremendous* sense of calm, comfort, and connection to not just the stunning calamity of nature, but the void, and their faith as an Aphotist.

If the Aphotist performs prayers or rituals during a rainstorm, the outcomes of these ceremonies shall be amplified – their fruits more nectarous and their fruition more clearly recognizable by the Aphotist.

METEOR SHOWERS

A divine performance by our mother, the void, the Aphotist can find tremendous power and energy in meteor showers. Occurring only a few dozen times a year, but not *always* observable when they occur, meteor showers are an *excellent* time for Aphotists to perform rituals and form a deeper connection to their beliefs as an Aphotist and to the void herself.

If the Aphotist performs prayers or rituals during a meteor shower, it is believed that the power of this event will carry over into any ceremonies that may be performed, resulting in *significantly* greater and more recognizable outcomes, blessings, and fruits.

HARVEST MOON

The last full moon before the beginning of autumn, the *harvest moon* in Aphotism represents the death of summer and the coming of the witching solstice.

As well, with summer's end and autumn's advent, winter is not far behind – another *powerful* time of year for the Aphotist, symbolically and spiritually. Like the void and the ocean's deeps – inhospitable, ethereal, and absent of warmth – winter represents darkness and the cold, *both* of which are attributes that the void and the deep ocean share in common.

If the Aphotist performs prayers or rituals during a harvest moon, they will find their connection to the void *drastically* intensified – as well, the outcomes of their ceremonies may be amplified, especially if these rituals employ natural magic or demonology.

TEMPESTS

Not a celebration of disaster, but an observation of the sheer power and potential for chaos that nature may *effortlessly* unleash upon the Earth, Aphotists recognize floods, hurricanes, tsunamis, and similar storms as opportunities to connect with nature and feel the Neptunian wrath of the seas from far away.

If the Aphotist performs prayers or rituals during a major event storm, they shall find their connection to the void *significantly* amplified – and, too, their occult ceremonies shall yield darker, sweeter fruit.

THE FOURTH CHAPTER

CALLED

THE APHOTIC ARTS

Though Aphotism by itself is a comprehensive and potent avenue of the Left-Hand Path, it is common for practitioners to embrace Aphotism's malleable and fluid nature by incorporating *secondary* occult arts into their rituals, beliefs, and spiritual studies.

ASTROMANCY

One of the most *powerful* arts that the Aphotist can add to their studies upon the Left-Hand Path, there is a tremendous wealth of knowledge to be gained from *astromancy* – the occult art of using the stars to divine the future and chart one's course forward.

In today's world, astromancy is a common art, but few would ever know it – horoscopes, natal charts, and predicting future events based on the positions of stars and the retrogrades of planets are *all* means by which we employ the ancient art of astromancy.

Though many Aphotists find success with utilizing these everyday astromantic tools, *most* of us prefer to use more dynamic means of consulting the stars for divination – methods such as astral projection, dream manipulation, liminal mirroring, or scrying.

HYDROMANCY

Uncommonly studied by today's occultists but an invaluable and quintessential tool in the Aphotist's arsenal, the Left-Hand Path art of *hydromancy* has empowered *millions* of practitioners, new and old.

Though there are many ways of practicing the art of hydromancy, its use in Aphotism is generally as a form of *meditation* – watching the reflections of the stars in a still body of water, or focusing on the waves and ripples of running water as a means of disassociating from the physical and exploring the psychospiritual. In doing so, the occultist may find it easier to attain clarity or peace with matters they would otherwise find stressful, dark, or confusing.

ONEIROMANCY

One of the core aspects of Aphotism's teachings is that darkness is *not* synonymous with pain – that it is an opportunity for growth and the attainment of wisdom, courage, and strength for those souls who dare take that first, tenebrous step into uncertainty.

A pleasant experience for every person at one time or another, *dreams* are often regarded as an escape from the chaos of life – that is, until those dreams lose their light and become *nightmares*. There are few people who would ever stop to wonder if their nightmares may have something beneficial to offer or teach them – luckily, Aphotists do not make this mistake, for we recognize the value of nightmares.

Though one does not need to induce nightmares, if they happen to *organically* occur, it would be wise to reflect on them upon waking – searching for any veiled messages or meanings that, if heeded, might ease life's tragedy, offer relief, or lead the Aphotist to the ambrosial fruits of otherworldly power that would have otherwise remained untasted, *forever*.

THE THIRD BOOK OF APHOTISM

CALLED THE

BOOK OF TIDES

Within the Book of Tides, you shall find all manner of philosophical information – it is an exploration of Aphotism's core spiritual beliefs and the ways in which we interpret life, death, magic, and faith.

This third pillar of The Abyssal Bible will bring to light everything that Aphotism believes regarding death, reincarnation, the nature of the human soul, life beyond humanity, and interdimensional planes of reality that could substantiate the metaphysical.

AMONGST ETERNITY

It is the misguided belief of many blind souls that what we can *immediately* see, quantify, or are able to comprehend is all that exists – that all of life and creation *must* fit snugly within the claustrophobic confines that modern society has agreed upon, and the average, weak person is too naïve to challenge.

On the Left-Hand Path of Aphotism, however, we believe that what can be immediately perceived is only a *scintilla* of reality – that with even our most advanced sciences and technologies, humanity has only beheld a nanoscopic speck of our universe, its secrets, and what may lie within its ancient depths.

We believe that all things are made possible within and through the void – life, death, and rebirth. The birth, toil, and death of intelligent civilizations, not unlike our own. That, if one delves far enough into our universe, they shall come across doorways that lead to *endless* other universes – and some of these other universes may even resemble the Heaven or Hell that we have come to know and fear on Earth.

One of the fundamental beliefs of Aphotism is that *everything* exists in the void – that somewhere, in some cold, dark recess of space and time, *anything* you can imagine *will* or already *does* exist. If our universe is infinite and forever expanding, then at some point, no matter how infinitesimal the odds, **every** possibility **will** eventually become a reality, and any entity you can imagine will or does exist. Hooved, horned, formless, or deformed – twisted creatures and forgotten shadows so deep and black that Hell itself would beg for light. Entities of such *monstrous* power that to call them a god would not only be wrong, but an insult to their omnipotence.

It is this belief in the ever-expanding nature of our universe – one of possibly *infinite* universes – that makes Aphotism stand out from other studies upon the Left-Hand Path. As well, our desire to uncover and commune with entities not yet documented by the ancient tomes and grimoires of our ancestors is another powerful tool in Aphotism's arsenal – one that works synergistically with our openness to the infinitude of the void and the universes within her.

The Aphotist is not limited by the commandments of corrupt faiths nor the bitter teachings of godless philosophies – we are not confined to the withered landscape of Earth in our pursuit of transcendental knowledge and power. The Aphotist does not have limits to their potential – our limits are a malleable, ever-shifting horizon, just like the horizons of our universe and the void herself. Unconstrained by an oppressive doctrine or guidelines that are meant to suppress the growth of its practitioners, Aphotism encourages its followers to broaden their interests to include the unknown – spirits, entities, realms, deities, and concepts that may exist *far* beyond the picked-over grimoires of yore and hierarchies that for *centuries* have been drained of their originality.

DEATH ≠ DEATH

On the Left-Hand Path of Aphotism, we believe in eternal life beyond death – that, once your physical body perishes, the *essence* of you shall be returned to the void to be reincarnated. By some Aphotists, this essence is thought of as the soul, and to others, it is consciousness – the immortal spark that makes us each a *remarkably* unique and sentient creature.

It is because of the benevolence of the void that we each were chosen to be born with the divine gift of *consciousness* – a gift that can **never** be returned, no matter what happens to your physical body. We believe that the physical body is not the person, but the *soul* is – that your soul experiences life through the physical body it leases, and when this physical body dies, the soul returns to the depths of the void until that fateful hour it has been slated for rebirth.

We believe that *all* things are made possible within and through the void – life, death, and rebirth. The dawn and extinction of intelligent civilizations not too dissimilar to our own. That, if one delves deep enough into the murky depths of our universe, they will uncover doorways that lead to *countless* other universes – some of which may even resemble the biblical Heaven and Hell that humankind has been utterly obsessed with for over two thousand years.

Though this notion of eternity is exhilarating to the Aphotist, it is usually a *terrifying* prospect to those who do not follow the Left-Hand Path – rather than being a source of inspiration or excitement, it tends to haunt the average person with a *profound* sense of dread and inescapable discomfort. In Aphotism, however, it is an *invaluable* source of comfort – a promise, of some strange sort, that the sorrows and petty theatrics of life will not only eventually come to an end, but that future lives and fates may await the Aphotist within the ageless depths of the void.

Our belief in eternal rebirth does not mean that the Aphotist eagerly anticipates death – contrarily, our belief in the transitory nature of death allows us to better appreciate the beauty of life, even during her darkest hours. Since Aphotists believe that we will experience life again, it is easier for us to stomach the suffering of life – pain, fear, sickness, violence, and *every* other malignant fruit that life shall force us each to eat. To us, this life is not our only chance to live and live well – to impact the world, make a positive change in society, and find true happiness.

As well, I believe the Aphotist possesses a unique ability that few, if any, religions offer – we can see and quantify the existence of our spiritual paradise *before* we die. We do not need to rely on creativity, hope, or imagination to paint a picture of what our paradise looks like. We *know* that it exists, and our proof is abundant – all that one must do is look up, and whether met by a fiery sun or midnight's stars, you, too, will believe that your life and this strange world upon which we dwell exists within the void.

THE MACHINE SOUL

It is no secret that the majority of religions believe in some form of an afterlife – Heaven and Hell are the two most commonly discussed, but there exist *thousands* of spiritual paradises amongst religions, new and old. In fact, the anticipation of an afterlife is arguably the most captivating facet *of* a religion, and it is what keeps practitioners of said faith from deviating too far from that religion's belief system.

There is an unspoken belief amongst the religious population that their actions *can* and *will* decide if their soul, upon death, will reach the paradise that their religion depicts. This implies one very simple but *extraordinary* idea: that **you** have control over where your soul goes, once you die. That life anew is not determined by a god or gods, but by how the practitioner lives their life – that the guidelines of one's religion are as much a *compass* as they are a rubric for living an honorable and exceptional life.

On the Left-Hand Path of Aphotism, we believe in and celebrate this idea – that your actions and how you caretake your soul in life shall determine your soul's destination upon death. Amongst Aphotists, this notion is often referred to as *the machine soul.*

A common misconception within a religious mind is that *their* god is the ultimate arbiter of their soul, and that no power is higher than the higher power they worship – and Aphotism disagrees. To us, the highest conceivable power is the void, for *nothing* can exist without her. A comparison I like to make while explaining this concept is between a city and a state – both of which have their own laws, edicts, and powers, but that power is not equal. A city can only exist within the confines of a state, but a state can exist without a city – and, too, the void would exist without a god or gods, but if gods exist, they can *only* exist within the dreamscape of the void.

The message here is not that gods are powerless or subservient to the void – rather, it is to clarify that, if gods *do* exist, they *only* exist because the void's existence allows them to. To Aphotists, this means that the laws of gods are secondary to those of the void, and that you have more control over the fate of your soul than you may realize – and, if this is true, then you have the *remarkable* opportunity to plot your soul's course and destination upon death.

On the Left-Hand Path of Aphotism, we regard the soul as a malleable essence that may be guided and programmed to follow a desired trajectory – much like a machine can be programmed to follow a set of prompts or commands that will allow it to reach a desired outcome. To an outsider, this may sound like the wheelhouse of gods – something that is *far* beyond the ability of a mere human to achieve. To Aphotists, however, the ability to direct the fate of one's soul is a feat of spiritual engineering that we celebrate and pursue in our embrace of Aphotism.

THE LIMINAL DOOR

An endless source of mystery and magic since the advent of civilization, we have *obsessed* ourselves with notions of the human soul – what it is, how to prove it exists, and, if it does, where it may reside when separated from its earthly vessel. There is no shortage of exciting ideas that have been amassed by religious minds over the centuries, but I believe that Aphotism's hypothesis is *indisputably* unique.

While many religions theorize that the soul *leaves* Earth to a faraway kingdom amongst the abyss, we believe it might exist in a dimension that overlaps ours – cohabitating in the same space and time, but in a realm we cannot perceive, except for when an anomaly occurs that we then refer to as a *haunting*.

You see, though Aphotism *does* believe in rebirth, we do not believe it happens instantaneously upon one's death – and why would it? It would be more than a bit arrogant to believe the void works at the snap of a mortal's finger to enact her divinity when we are likely a nanoscopic drop in her bucket, and what we would perceive as eternity is no more than the rapid ticking of the seconds hand on her clock.

The cyclical order of death, time, and rebirth is not latched to our trivial mortal customs – the minutes, hours, days, and years as we believe them to be are absolutely irrelevant to any intelligent civilization, god, or deity, for they are our unique human means of attempting to rationalize the passage of time. To the void as a sentient creator, neither an hour nor a year exists – they are *our* delineations. In our time, this transitory period of rebirth could be *thousands* of years, but to the void, a fleeting blink of an eye.

We believe that, during this ephemeral period that follows one's death, the soul will remain where the body perished, but in a dimension that overlaps the realm of the living until it has been prepared to be reborn elsewhere within the void – and, during this period of time, the spiritual and earthly planes may interact with each other. Typically, this interaction will occur somewhere the deceased has a *powerful* emotional attachment to – their home, by the side of their living spouse, or even where they lost their life. When a spiritually sensitive person enters said environment, they are able to sense the presence of the spirit, and the spirit is then able to interact with the person – *congratulations*, you have a haunting.

As you navigate the mountains and malebolgia of life and the Left-Hand Path, you do so through an *endless* sea of listless souls – each one awaiting the hour they will be whisked away from the terminal of the dead into the dreamscape of the void. There is a subjacent kingdom entangled within this grey, mechanical plane of existence – a world that exists in tandem with ours at all times, even if it is rarely seen, felt, or quantified by the majority of people. The devoted Aphotist, *however*, may interact with this spiritual dimension with relative ease, for they have opened themselves to the void – and, in turn, the void shall serve as their liminal doorway to the spiritual realms and dimensions beyond this Earth.

THE FOURTH BOOK OF APHOTISM

CALLED THE

BOOK OF ECHOES

Within the Book of Echoes, you shall be provided with several prewritten, ready-to-recite hymns and prayers, each one devoted to the celebration of the void and the empowerment of the faithful Aphotist.

This final pillar of The Abyssal Bible will offer you a warmer and less analytical finale that, hopefully, leaves you with a sense of comfort, empowerment, and excitement in the Left-Hand Path of Aphotism.

THE VOID, OUR MOTHER

From your cradle I came, and to it, I shall return

when my ghost grows weary and old – when

darkness devours the light of the sun,

and this world grows black

and cold – hark, dear void, my vaporous mother,

and accept these gossamer words!

HER ANCIENT DEEPS

To she whose strange and ancient heights
reflect upon drear oceans deep – roiling, black,
and thundering folds, whispering to me
like the mountains old – lend to me your cosmic
sight, and empower me with your
Acheronian might.

RITE OF UNBINDING

Hark, dear abyss, and accept this rite!

Cast o'er me your starry light, and illuminate
this dreadful night – free me from the shadows
that bind and fetter my soul with
their deathless plight.

IN ELDRITCH SHADOWS

And to the abyss, this arcane rite!

In eldritch shadows, I walk with you through
worlds and realms unseen – dimensions beyond
most mortal sight, where all manner
of spirits convene.

THE MARINER'S LIGHT

Hail she whose phthalo tides surge deep
and roll, and heave like mountains green – hail
she who gives the mariners light, o'
pendulous sphere that haunts
the night!

ODE TO THE ABYSS

O' my darkest void, heed this Hadean prayer!

I, _____, am a constellated apostle
of the abyss – an Aphotist, sheathed in the silken
vapors of your eternity and illuminated
by the dying breaths of a thousand
forgotten suns!

THE APHOTIST'S PRAYER

*I, _____, am a herald of the void
on Earth – a resolute Aphotist, safeguarded
within the deathless shadows of the abyss
and illuminated by her Promethean
constellations!*

THE APHOTIST

It is my hope that, after reading *The Abyssal Bible,* you not only have a newfound appreciation for the void but have found applicable value in the beliefs and teachings of Aphotism – and, too, that you are able to apply these teachings to your journey upon the Left-Hand Path in a way that brings you power.

I believe that, if *truly* embraced, the void will bring joy, comfort, and power to *every* person regardless of their religious beliefs or prejudices. The void is an *indisputable* fact of life – she is the architect of all creation, and the canvas upon which humanity casts its brushstrokes in an attempt to find meaning in this bizarre, nebulous theatre that we call reality.

On the Left-Hand Path of Aphotism, occultists are given the tools to create the reality **they** desire – to etch out a life that brings them peace, purpose, and power instead of the bleak suffering and stifling of potential that much of today's world advocates as the status quo. The 21st century does not favor free thinkers nor those that refuse to fall in line with the preapproved religions or philosophies that society has deemed acceptable – with this, I felt that it was necessary for me to present Aphotism to the world.

As an apostle of the void, your potential will *never* again be restricted by the limitations of this mortal plane – the limits of what you can achieve are vast, vaporous, and *unfathomable*, just like the edgeless kingdom of our mother amongst the stars, the void.

OTHER PUBLICATIONS

The Infernal Gospel

The Goetia Devils

The Goetia Hymns

The Satanic Philosopher

Ars Diabolica

Ars Animarum

Ars Aeterna

Ars Sanguinea

Ars Exitialis

The Hierophant of Hell – Coming Soon

You may find us on Facebook, as well as on Etsy, where we offer our world-renowned demonological grimoires, occult antiques, and *numerous* Left-Hand Path oddities.

For business inquiries, please use the messaging feature on Etsy and contact us directly – if your inquiries regard wholesale purchase of our paperback books, we cannot directly assist you – it **is** something that we offer, but it must be done via Amazon KDP's business services, and we cannot facilitate the process in any meaningful way.

Etsy: TheInfernalCircle

Made in United States
Troutdale, OR
04/29/2024

19538610R00086